*"When I was a new Christian 50 years ago, I read two little booklets by John Stott on personal evangelism that changed my life. Matt Smethurst has written a short book on the same subject that is every bit as good as those older essays, but of course far more up to date. Read it—it could change your life!"*

**Timothy Keller**, Redeemer City to City

*"Matt Smethurst has given God's people a tremendously valuable resource: something to help prepare us for evangelism. He addresses topics that are often skipped over or assumed in evangelism training. And he does so with excellent prose and gospel grace."*

**Randy Newman**, senior fellow for apologetics and evangelism, The C. S. Lewis Institute; author, *Questioning Evangelism*

*"Jumping to the 'how' in evangelism is the norm. But Matt Smethurst prepares us for the jump by unpacking why we should jump in the first place . . . and it's fabulously helpful in every way. This book aligns your heart to answer evangelism's 'why,' and then graciously kicks your behind to get involved for the glory of God."*

**Shelby Abbott**, campus minister, Cru; podcast/radio host, FamilyLife; author

"Matt Smethurst has written a helpful book for what seems like the bulk of us—those who want to share our faith, but haven't quite gotten there yet. He gives us a view of the gospel we proclaim, the obstacles we encounter on the way, and the God who overcomes them. I am happy to commend this handy resource to ministry leaders and anyone looking to get after the work God has given the church."

**Derek Rishmawy**, campus minister, Reformed University Fellowship; co-host, *Mere Fidelity* podcast

"Few people can write a warm, winsome book on evangelism while still maintaining biblical faithfulness, but Matt Smethurst has pulled it off. Matt is a player-coach who walks alongside us, outlining the foundational components of sharing our faith and never forgetting that evangelism is part of every faithful believer's life. This book will instruct the fearless and invigorate the fearful."

**J. Mack Stiles**, director, Messenger Ministries; author, *Evangelism* and *Marks of the Messenger*

"Packed with pastoral wisdom, theological clarity, and a contagious zeal—both for Christ and for the lost. I can't think of a better short encouragement toward evangelism. Read it with friends, and get sharing!"

**Glen Scrivener**, evangelist and author

"Every Christian would love to tell their friends about Jesus. So why don't we do it more often? It's certainly not due to lack of opportunities. What if the barriers are not so much what's outside us but what's inside? Matt Smethurst's book will remove barriers and motivate you to share your faith—as the title promises! It will be life-changing for you, and for the friends you tell about Jesus."

**Sam Chan**, City Bible Forum, Australia; author, *Evangelism in a Skeptical World* and *How To Talk about Jesus*

"This is a delightful book on evangelism! Matt Smethurst focuses on the crucial topic of how to prepare for witness—before the opportunity arrives. His writing is clear, concise, compelling, and insightful. This is an important contribution on a very important subject."

**Rebecca Manley Pippert**, author, *Out of the Saltshaker and Into the World* and *Stay Salt*

"People tend to overcomplicate things. We can be so busy looking for the Bible study plan that we forget to study our Bibles. We form well-intentioned discipleship pathways that are more of a maze than a map. That's why I love this book by Matt Smethurst. It doesn't dodge the challenges we face, but it does something many evangelism books don't: it shows the simplicity and wonder of the gospel. Matt takes a step back to explain how any believer can be prepared to share this good news with both strangers and friends. Read this—and put what you read into practice. It's really that simple."

**Ed Stetzer**, executive director, Wheaton College Billy Graham Center; dean, School of Mission, Ministry, and Leadership

"I must confess that sometimes I don't share my faith when I should. But this little book is not designed to make me ashamed of myself (I don't need help in that department), but to help me do better. If you are a Christian who never wavers on this front, don't bother reading this book: you don't need it. Otherwise read it thoughtfully and gratefully."

**D. A. Carson**, cofounder and theologian-at-large, The Gospel Coalition; emeritus professor of New Testament, Trinity Evangelical Divinity School

# BEFORE YOU
# SHARE *your* FAITH

## FIVE WAYS TO BE
## EVANGELISM READY

### MATT SMETHURST

a division of 10ofthose.com

First published in Great Britain in 2022

The right of Matt Smethurst to be identified as the Author of this Work
has been asserted by him in accordance with the Copyright, Designs
and Patents Act 1988.

British Library Cataloguing in Publication Data
A record for this book is available from the British Library

ISBN: 978-1-913896-84-3

Designed and typeset by Pete Barnsley (CreativeHoot.com)

Printed in Denmark by Nørhaven

10Publishing, a division of 10ofthose.com
Unit C, Tomlinson Road, Leyland, PR25 2DY, England

Email: info@10ofthose.com
Website: www.10ofthose.com

3 5 7 10 8 6 4

*To Dan Flynn, who was gospel-centered before it was cool, and who showed a young college kid that sharing Christ is the most exhilarating privilege on earth.*

# CONTENTS

# INTRODUCTION:

# NOT YOUR TYPICAL EVANGELISM BOOK

I have a love-hate relationship with evangelism books.

On the one hand, they have helped me immensely. It's surely no coincidence that in the seasons of life when I've been most deliberate about sharing Christ with others, a good book on the topic has invigorated me. And vice versa: in the sluggish seasons, it's usually the case that I haven't pondered the subject in a while.

I'm quite skilled, you see, at avoiding things that are good for me. Exercise. Kale. Books on this topic. (Come to think of it, evangelism books can sometimes taste like kale.)

The main reason I'm tempted to avoid evangelism books, though, is because they reawaken something I'd rather keep suppressed: a low-level guilt, humming beneath the surface, that whispers: *You, Matt, are a lousy and inconsistent evangelist.*

And here I am writing a book on the topic! The gall! Except, I'm not. I'm actually doing something a bit different.

This is not a handbook of evangelistic jujitsu tips. I'll leave that to more able voices. This volume is about getting ready to open your mouth at all. It's about the preparation for the conversation.

In a previous book, *Before You Open Your Bible*,[1] I observed that how we approach things matters in a huge way. The world of sports is an obvious example—and a general analogy for life. Whether we're talking about a soccer player during warm-ups or a runner at the starting line, an athlete's simple approach can make all the difference.

Many evangelism books—including some excellent ones—start a little too downstream for me. I need help further up and further back, because I am so often stuck at the water's edge, unsure and immobilized, not quite ready to dive in.

Sometimes the problem is the inertia that comes with feeling out of practice—and the aforementioned guilt, or at least the lack of confidence, accompanying such a feeling. Other times it's simply the age-old presence of fear, or perhaps more accurately, the absence of love. My view of God can shrivel so much that it makes humans look inflated and intimidating.[2]

I don't know why you picked up this book, or if you did at all. (Perhaps someone shoved it into your unsuspecting hands.) But regardless of your reason for reading, here we are, exploring evangelism together. My hope is that the Holy Spirit would use these pages to ready your mind, and energize your heart, so that you joyfully and expectantly brag about the One who has changed your life.

Nothing is more worth talking about. And nothing is easier to stay silent about.

The remedy for this spiritual dilemma? I believe it may be hidden in what happens *before we share our faith*.

1

# GRASP THE GOSPEL

Among the preludes to sharing your faith that I am commending to you, this one tops the list. Why? Because without it, there is no list. You cannot do evangelism if you do not grasp the *evangel*, the good news of Christianity.

Let's face it: the word "gospel" gets thrown around somewhat loosely in Christian conversations today—so much so that its weighty meaning can get lost, or at least muffled. To grasp the good news of the gospel, then, we must internalize the significance of that word "news." After all, this is what separates Christianity from every other religion. Christianity is not fundamentally an ethical code, or good *advice*. It is, above all, an announcement of good *news*.

You don't need to go to seminary in order to grasp the gospel. You don't need to be in ministry to grasp the gospel. You don't even need to have been a Christian for five minutes in order to grasp the gospel well enough to convey it to others.

All you need to understand is that two thousand years ago, an invasion took place. Heaven came to earth in the person of Jesus, and he inaugurated a whole new kingdom.[3] For thirty-three years, he lived a life of unflinching, perfect faithfulness to God the Father. In other words, he lived the life that, try as we might, we cannot live. And because he loves us, he died the death that we deserved to die. As a believer in Jesus, I can know that on the cross he was treated as if he had lived my sinful life, so that I might be treated as if I have lived his righteous life.

And then Jesus was buried. Until he wasn't—because three days later, he got up and walked out of his tomb. Now everyone who turns from their rebellion—whether of the plainly wicked or subtly "religious" variety—and trusts in Jesus is united to him in this life and the next. Believers will one day be resurrected in new bodies fit for a new, resurrected earth. We will enter into the joy of our triune Lord—Father, Son, and Holy Spirit—and will rule under him as kings and queens of the universe, forever.

In a skeptical age, this may all sound far-fetched, like a fairy tale for gullible kids. *Too good to be true.* But this news is entirely true. It just isn't deserved—indeed, it isn't fair. As one song phrases it, "Why should I gain from his reward? I cannot give an answer."[4]

But mercy is never fair. That's why it's called mercy.

## ONE GOSPEL, TWO ANGLES

I live in Richmond, Virginia, and there are things about my city—size, layout, population density, and so on—that I can best learn from the vantage point of an airplane. There are plenty of other things, though, that I can better learn by walking down Broad Street. Both perspectives are helpful, even necessary, for understanding Richmond. A street-level view without an aerial perspective to frame it, or an aerial view without a street-level perspective to fill it out, will inevitably yield a truncated frame of reference. Sure, we are just talking geography—Richmond's history and culture, for example, must be learned by other means—but a failure to see the city from various angles creates a one-dimensional, distorted outlook. Not to mention an impoverished appreciation for the area in all its fullness.

Likewise, the gospel can be profitably observed from two biblical vantage points: "in the air" and "on the ground."[5] Just as there are not two capital cities in Virginia, so there are not two gospels. There is one, which we can marvel at from two angles.

The gospel "in the air" is the sweeping story, from Genesis to Revelation, that can be summarized in a few plot points (for example, creation, fall, redemption, and new creation). The gospel "on the ground," meanwhile, fleshes out how this epic narrative becomes good news for sinners like us (for example, by looking at God, humanity, Christ, and our response).

At the outset of this chapter, I offered a brief summary of the gospel story. But we can fill it out even more. Perhaps one way to synthesize the *best* of these complementary perspectives— both "in the air" and "on the ground," both "wide lens" and "zoom lens"—is to consider the gospel story in four movements: the Ruler, the

Revolt, the Rescue, and the Response. I hope that this deeper dive will provide a rich context from which to share your faith.

## THE RULER

"In the beginning, God . . ." (Gen. 1:1). The Bible opens with history's most basic statement about reality.

God created, sustains, and rules everything that exists. Contrary to cultural misconceptions, he is not Santa in the sky, nor a cosmic vending machine, nor an irritable drill sergeant, nor a deadbeat dad. He is the King of glory and the Lord of love. In fact, he is an eternal community of persons, a *Father* loving his *Son* in the joy of the *Holy Spirit*. And because this loving and joyful God is Trinity—one God forever existing in three persons—love is at the heart of the universe.[6]

This triune God made humanity—you and me—in his image to know and enjoy his love. So we were made *by* God (which means he alone owns us) and *for* God (which means he alone satisfies us). Human beings were custom-designed to find meaning and fulfillment and life in our Creator above all else—above success, above popularity, above recreation, above romance, above *self*.

Now, is that the story of your life—being totally satisfied in your Maker and treasuring him above everything? It certainly isn't the story of mine.

What happened?

## THE REVOLT

We look for love in all the wrong places, because something has gone terribly wrong in our hearts. This echoes what happened when our first parents, Adam and Eve, turned their backs on God and chose to call the shots themselves,

> *THE TENTACLES OF SIN HAVE DEFORMED OUR HEARTS AND DISORDERED OUR LOVES.*

fracturing his creation and plunging his image-bearers into an ocean of sin. Instead of living for our Maker, we live for ourselves. The tentacles of sin have deformed our hearts and disordered our loves. Every one of us has rebelled, by both nature and choice, against the Lord of love.

It's easy to think of sin as a relatively minor thing—outward naughtiness perhaps, or a kind of heavenly parking ticket. But when the Bible talks about sin, it's talking about cosmic treason—an insurrection against heaven itself.

It is vital that we grasp at least two truths about the nature of sin.

First, sin is *more relational than behavioral*. When Adam and Eve rebelled against God, it wasn't just a behavioral boo-boo; it was a heart-level betrayal. We've cheated on our Maker, which is why Israel's sin in the Old Testament is so often cast in terms of spiritual adultery. We've desperately sought to build our lives around other things—anything—but him. We've taken good gifts and turned them into stand-ins for the Giver.

Second, sin is *more vertical than horizontal*. Its horizontal effects can be devastating, but sin is fundamentally a vertical problem. David, the "man after God's own heart," confesses well the predicament of us all:

> *For I know my transgressions,*
> *and my sin is ever before me.*
> *Against you, you only, have I sinned*
> *and done what is evil in your sight*
> *(Ps. 51:3–4; cf. Gen. 39:9; Luke 15:21).*

Here's something fascinating: "sin" is the only noun in the English language that is *larger* in its singular form. "Sin" is a bigger category than "sins." At the deepest level, then, we are not sinners because we sin—we sin because we are sinners.[7]

But it gets worse. Ponder this: the result of our me-ism and idolatry is nothing less than the creation of a catastrophic chasm between us and God. "Your iniquities have separated you from your God," the prophet Isaiah declares, "your sins have hidden his face from you so that he does not hear" (Isa. 59:2, NIV). We have bucked God's design for us, his image-bearers, and so we are severed from the ultimate Source of life and love. And when we die, it's time for justice: "It is appointed for man to die once, and after that comes judgment" (Heb. 9:27).

As a result of our sin, we are justly under God's wrath—his holy and settled opposition to evil. "If God is for us, who can be against us?" Paul asks believers (Rom. 8:31). But the reverse, for those outside of Christ, is also true: if God is against you, who can be for you?

In grasping the gospel, then, how good do you have to be to enter heaven? Here's the staggering answer: *as good as God*. Only persons whom God considers perfect can live with him forever.

This need for moral perfection, of course, is everlastingly bad news. Left to our own merit, we are standing on the precipice of a hopeless future in hell—not just God's absence, but the presence of his right and good justice.

Here's how Paul explains it to the Ephesians:

> *And you were dead in the trespasses and sins in which you once walked, following the course of this world, following the prince of the power of the air, the spirit that is now at work in the sons of disobedience—among whom we all once lived in the passions of our flesh, carrying out the desires of the body and the mind, and were by nature children of wrath, like the rest of mankind (Eph. 2:1–3).*

Instead of the credits rolling, though, Paul continues: *"But . . ."*

Have you ever thought about the fact that your entire eternity hangs on this one little word?

## THE RESCUE

Something happened in history to change the trajectory for those who rely on Jesus for salvation, and here's the decisive "but":

> But God, being rich in mercy, because of the great love with which he loved us, even when we were dead in our trespasses, made us alive together with Christ—by grace you have been saved (Eph. 2:4–5).

After centuries of rebellion by God's people, God's Son—the second person of the eternal Trinity—became an embryo, a baby, a teenager, a man. We couldn't get to God, so God came to us (Heb. 2:14–15). For thirty-three years, the carpenter from Nazareth lived a life of uninterrupted devotion and obedience to his heavenly Father. He prayed a lot of prayers, but never once a prayer of confession, because he never had any sin to confess.

Jesus lived the life of moral perfection that Adam failed to live, that Israel failed to live, and that you and I have failed to live.

And the Bible says Jesus became "obedient to the point of death, even death on a cross"

(Phil. 2:8). The One who made the law kept it, and then died for those who had broken it. The law-maker became the law-keeper and died in the place of law-breakers.[8]

We have now reached the white-hot center of the Christian faith: the death of Jesus Christ. On the cross God punished his Son, who is perfect, for the sins of those who are not.

But that's not the only thing that occurred. If all God did was cancel our sin, that would have simply brought us back to zero.

Think about it this way: there are eighty-two games in a National Basketball Association regular season. No team has ever achieved a perfect season—one without any losses. "But wait," some fan might object. "My team's record is currently 0-0. That's a perfect season—we haven't lost any games!"

To which we would rightly roll our eyes. "Your" team hasn't lost *because they haven't played all their games*. To have a perfect season you must never lose and always win—right through to the very last game.

In the Garden of Eden, Adam and Eve had a moral record, as it were, of 0-0. They hadn't sinned, so they were "undefeated." But neither had they achieved a lifetime of righteousness, so it wasn't a "perfect season." And when they turned from God, they became spiritually bankrupt. They plummeted to 0-82, the moral record we now inherit.

However, in the middle of history, one man amassed an unprecedented record: 82-0.

Continuing the illustration, here's the point: if Jesus *only* paid for our sins, our moral record would be 0-0. But on the cross, Jesus didn't just absorb our eighty-two losses; he also gave believers his eighty-two victories, certified by his empty tomb (Rom. 4:23–25). So our record shifts, in an instant, from 0-82 to 82-0. In the eyes of a holy God, it's now as if we've done nothing to offend him *and* everything to please him.

Paul puts it like this, referring to Christ: "God made him who had no sin to be sin for us, so that in him we might become the righteousness of God" (2 Cor. 5:21, NIV). To reiterate, on the cross God treated Christ as if he had lived a believer's sinful life, so that he could treat us as if we had lived Christ's spotless life. No wonder theologians call this "the sweet exchange."

What does this mean practically as we grasp the gospel for ourselves and others? Well, in the words of the Puritan Richard Sibbes, "There is more mercy in Christ than sin in us."[9] No matter who you are or what you've done, hear the magnificent news: there is more mercy in Jesus than sin in you.

> *NO MATTER WHO YOU ARE OR WHAT YOU'VE DONE, HEAR THE MAGNIFICENT NEWS: THERE IS MORE MERCY IN JESUS THAN SIN IN YOU.*

In our cultural moment, it is vital to grasp that Jesus didn't merely die to boost our self-esteem or to set a moral example. Such a perspective, however well-meaning, domesticates what he did. He stooped to take our place on the cross because we scramble to take his place on the throne. I love the way John Stott explains it:

*The concept of substitution may be said to lie at the heart of both sin and salvation. For the essence of sin is man substituting himself for God, while the essence of salvation is God substituting himself for man. Man asserts himself against God and puts himself where only God deserves to be; God sacrifices himself for man and puts himself where only man deserves to be. Man claims prerogatives that belong to God alone; God accepts penalties that belong to man alone.*[10]

Amen. And yet we must be careful, when presenting the gospel, not to leave Jesus hanging on the cross.

After his death, his brutalized corpse was placed in a "secure" tomb (Matt. 27:65–66), never to be heard from again. Except, he *was* heard from again—because the power of death could not suppress the Author of life (Acts 2:24; cf. 3:15). And so, as he had promised, on the third day he exited the tomb.

Again, as we prepare to share our faith, the resurrection is not an "add-on" to the gospel story—because without it, there is no gospel story. In raising Jesus from the dead, God was publicly affirming that his sacrifice on the cross had been accepted, a just and complete payment for sin. If on Good Friday redemption's check was signed, on Easter Sunday the check cleared.

And one day, this same Jesus—who died and rose and ascended to heaven and intercedes for his people—is going to make a comeback. Those who have not trusted him will receive justice; those who *have* will receive mercy. Our ultimate hope as Christians is not evacuation from this earth, but the restoration of this earth.[11] God's

> *OUR ULTIMATE HOPE IS NOT EVACUATION FROM THIS EARTH, BUT THE RESTORATION OF THIS EARTH. GOD'S REDEEMED PEOPLE WILL INHERIT A REMADE WORLD, UNMARRED BY THE SCOURGE OF SIN.*

redeemed people will inherit a remade world, unmarred by the scourge of sin. This is why the Scriptures portray our future home in concrete, material terms—"new heavens and a new earth" (Isa. 65:17; cf. 2 Pet. 3:13; Rev. 21:1–4). Contrary to popular belief, we won't be floating around playing golden harps with chubby angels. We'll be running and working and playing and singing and laughing and resting and reveling in the endless wonders of our good and beautiful God.

## THE RESPONSE

When you pass through a highway toll and interact with the person in the booth, is it a meaningful experience? Not exactly. It's a business transaction: you pay the money; they raise the bar. You do your part; they do theirs.

Becoming a Christian, friend, is *not* like this. It's not a cold transaction. It's more like getting married—an intensely personal union. You throw yourself on Jesus for mercy; he catches you and never lets go.

So, as we grasp this gospel we long to impart to others, we can be ready to answer the most important question one could ask: *What must I do to be right with God?*

First, we *turn* from sin. We're skilled at confessing the evil of others, but we should be most devastated by our own. This is the meaning of repentance—changing your mind and doing an "about-face," a 180-degree pivot from living for yourself.

Second, we *trust* Jesus Christ. We say "no" to sin and "yes" to him, embracing what he has accomplished for us and his invincible promise to forgive. Repentance and faith, after all, are two sides of the same coin.[12]

Third, we *treasure* Jesus. Now, technically this is not a third step—it's the outcome of the second. But it's worth spelling out because many "accept" Christ the way I might accept, say, a root canal. Grasping the gospel, though, entails *embracing* Jesus as your Lord and Savior and Treasure.

What this means, among other things, is that Jesus Christ is infinitely more than a get-out-of-hell-free pass. He is a living person to follow, worship, cherish, and enjoy. Indeed, knowing him is the only way to be restored to a right relationship with the God for whom we were made (John 14:6; 17:3). Through him we can experience the joy of forgiveness, the help of the Holy Spirit, and the hope of the world to come.

> JESUS CHRIST IS INFINITELY MORE THAN A GET-OUT-OF-HELL-FREE PASS. HE IS A LIVING PERSON TO FOLLOW, WORSHIP, CHERISH, AND ENJOY.

No person is saved by getting baptized, going to church, retweeting Christian sentiments, praying a prayer, signing a card, walking an aisle, or throwing a pinecone into the fire at summer camp. The critical question facing each of us blows right past everything outward, for it is laser-aimed at the heart: *Are you, right now, relying on Jesus alone for your standing before God?*

The gospel demands a response. "Now is the day of salvation," Paul insists (2 Cor. 6:2). In sharing our faith, let's urge people to respond to the claims of Christ—and so bring them to that eternally consequential point of decision.

This is the greatest story ever told—and anybody can get in on it. Who are you going to invite?

2

# CHECK YOUR CONTEXT

"Jesus is an American god!"

Though a missionary overseas at the time, I was unprepared for this answer. I had just asked my new friend, an educated college student, what he knew about Jesus Christ. I certainly was not expecting him to recite the Nicene Creed. What startled me, though, was the confidence with which he answered. I might as well have asked the name of his school.

Now, imagine if I had promptly replied by explaining that Jesus loves him and died for his sins and rose again so that he could go to heaven forever.

*What does that have to do with me?* he would've rightly wondered. *We're not in America.*

Cutting to the glories of Good Friday and Resurrection Sunday may well have made me feel valiant in the moment—*I am not ashamed of the gospel!*—but it would have been foolish, even unloving. Because first I needed to clear away the static in the air.

## WHO'S THE AUDIENCE?

In order to share our faith effectively, we need to know our audience. And not only know someone's name and maybe where they go to school or what they do for a living—but, as the saying goes, "where are they coming from?"

Now, on one level, we should be careful not to *overemphasize* humanity's various differences. Regardless of culture, ethnicity, language, or background, a common denominator unites us: having been made in God's image, we have all rebelled against him and need rescue from our deserved plight. The good news of the Bible, then, is applicable to every society because the bad news is relevant to every sinner.

But we also should not *underemphasize* cultural differences, as if they have no bearing on how people hear the message. And this is not just a principle for missionaries in far-flung places.

In the modern West, as I'm sure you've noticed, things are not as they were just a few years ago. Previously, you could pretty much assume the other person was coming into a conversation on spiritual matters *furnished*— with a basic understanding of a creator God; of sin as breaking the Ten Commandments; of the Bible as a respected resource; of life after death in heaven; and so on.

> WE MUST TAKE CARE TO LEAN IN AND LISTEN WELL, TO CLIMB INTO THE OTHER PERSON'S WAY OF SEEING AND INHABITING THE WORLD.

Clearly, those days are over. In a secular, post-Christian age, we cannot presume any basic assumptions in those we are trying to reach with the gospel.[13] So we must take care to lean in and listen well, to climb into the other person's way of seeing and inhabiting the world. Otherwise, we will be speaking about terms—even biblical ones—that will be simply misunderstood or rejected outright.

- *God loves you* is great news, but meaningless if you don't understand the nature of God (or for that matter, love).

- *You are a sinner* is true, but meaningless if you don't know what sin is or don't feel that badly about it.

- *You need a Savior* is true, but meaningless if you don't grasp what you need to be saved from.

- *The Bible says . . .* is great, unless the Bible is considered an archaic, patriarchal collection of fairy tales.

## TO CONTEXTUALIZE OR NOT TO CONTEXTUALIZE, THAT IS NOT THE QUESTION

This is where discussions concerning (big-word alert) *contextualization* often go awry. How should ambassadors of Christ communicate an unchanging message in ever-changing contexts?

When it comes to the gospel, we don't need to dress it up in order to make it cool. We need to break it down in order to make it clear. *That is the purpose of studying your surrounding culture in light of God's Word.* What are people's prevailing values, hopes, and fears? How does the gospel story both fulfill their deepest longings and subvert their most cherished idols?

> WHEN IT COMES TO THE GOSPEL, WE DON'T NEED TO DRESS IT UP IN ORDER TO MAKE IT COOL. WE NEED TO BREAK IT DOWN IN ORDER TO MAKE IT CLEAR.

Such questions are not original to modern missiologists. Rewind the clock two thousand years and even the Son of God did not engage lost persons in a one-size-fits-all manner. He took a certain approach with self-righteous Pharisees (e.g., Mark 12:13–17), another with skeptical Sadducees (e.g., Mark 12:18–27), and another with notorious sinners (e.g., Mark 2:13–17).

Paul did likewise: in Acts 17, he took one approach with biblically literate Jews in Thessalonica (vv. 1–9) and Berea (vv. 10–15), but a different approach entirely with pagan Greeks in Athens (vv. 16–34). Was the apostle confused? Cowardly? Spiritually schizophrenic? Not at all. He was simply dialed into his various contexts, and willing to adapt accordingly. We aren't left to psychoanalyze him, either. He laid out his strategy:

> *For though I am free from all, I have made myself a servant to all, that I might win more of them. To the Jews I became as a Jew, in order to win Jews. To those under the law I became as one under the law (though not being myself under the law) that I might win those under the law. To those outside the law I became as one outside the law (not being outside the law of God but under the law of Christ) that I might win those outside the law. To the weak I became weak, that I might win the weak. I have become all things to all people, that by all means I might save some. I do it all for the sake of the gospel, that I may share with them in its blessings (1 Cor. 9:19–23).*

In claiming to be "free from all," Paul meant that he didn't answer finally to people. Elsewhere, he put it pointedly:

> *For am I now seeking the approval of man, or of God? Or am I trying to please man? If I*

*were still trying to please man, I would not be a*
*servant of Christ (Gal. 1:10).*

And yet, even though Paul didn't answer to people, he did *accommodate* to them. Why? To remove any barriers that might make it harder for someone to have a direct encounter with Christ. Reflecting on 1 Corinthians 9:19, the Protestant reformer Martin Luther captured the dynamic well: "A Christian is a perfectly free lord of all, subject to none. [And] a Christian is a perfectly dutiful servant of all, subject to all."[14]

Three hundred years after Luther, in 1854, a young British missionary named Hudson Taylor arrived on the shores of China. As he started traveling around and seeking to share Christ, he quickly found that the Chinese people were distracted by his foreignness; they were more interested in his Western outfits and manners than in hearing his message. This frustrating discovery prompted Taylor to change not his gospel, but his game plan.

What did the missionary do? He started living like a Chinese man. This included not only wearing Chinese garb, but even dyeing his hair black and wearing it in a traditional Chinese braid. Why was he contextualizing like this? Was it to deceive people about his own heritage? Or to feel like an ancient hipster? Of course not. It was so that he would not *himself* be a distraction from his message of gospel grace.

Hudson Taylor went on to spend fifty-one years in China, and the little organization he founded became the largest missions agency in the world. Missionaries from China Inland Mission eventually reached every province in the country, establishing roughly 125 schools and seeing, according to some reports, over 18,000 conversions to Jesus Christ.

My point is not that Taylor's particular approach would be wise now—it probably wouldn't. But note the gospel fruit that was born from one man's sacrificial choice to creatively adapt to his context—to relinquish some of his own cultural preferences and, by so doing, remove barriers to sharing Christ.

It is easy, when reading 1 Corinthians 9:19–23, to so fixate on "I became . . . I became . . . I became" that we overlook what *grounds* the refrain: "I serve." Fundamentally, good contextualizing is not about being cool; it is about being a servant. It's about creatively laboring to make the message of the cross and the joy of the resurrection crystal clear.

It does not take a seminary degree to see what Paul was pursuing in his daily life. *The* thing that drove him—to flex, to adapt, to sacrifice—was his paramount passion to see lost persons brought to Christ: "I do it all for the sake of the gospel" (v. 23).

## WHAT'S AT STAKE?

To be clear, these statements from Paul are not meant to be infinitely elastic. He is stretching as far as he can to reach the lost, but he's not going to compromise truth to get there. Nor is he advocating that we indulge in sinful behavior in order to be relatable. "All things to all people" means all *legitimate* things. Paul is not saying, "To the gossips I became a gossip; to the drunkards I became a drunkard; to the cannibals I became a cannibal." But he *is* saying, in essence, "I move as near to other people as I possibly can. I flex and adapt to meet them on their turf—as far as truth and wisdom allow."

I think the first words in 1 Corinthians 9:20 represent one of the most incredible statements Paul ever made: "To the Jews I became as a Jew." *What? He was already a Jew.* This would be like me saying, "Here is my grand evangelistic strategy: to Americans from Virginia I become as an American from Virginia; to lovers of candy I become as a lover of candy."

What's going on?

It's not that Paul is ashamed of his ethnic identity; in other places he refers warmly to "my fellow Jews." But he can propose this counterintuitive concept—"to the Jews I become as a Jew"—because *he wears his Jewishness loosely.* It's almost like he can speak of putting it on and taking it off—not because it doesn't matter, nor because he's in denial, but because his most fundamental identity is no longer, "I am a Jew, a Hebrew of Hebrews, of the tribe of Benjamin" (cf. Phil. 3:5), but rather, "I am a disciple, the chief of sinners, of the people of Jesus."

I can think of two examples of this principle at work in Paul's own life. One is a passing reference in Acts 18 to Paul cutting his hair because he was "under a vow" (v. 18). We don't know the exact nature of the vow, but it was some kind of Jewish ritual, perhaps similar to the Nazirite vow in Numbers 6.

The other, more complicated, example is Acts 16:3:

*Paul wanted Timothy to accompany him, and*
*he took him and circumcised him because of the*
*Jews who were in those places, for they all knew*
*that [Timothy's] father was a Greek.*

Now, if you're familiar with the Book of Romans and especially Galatians, then you ought to be a little puzzled—if not scandalized—when you read that. Because in Galatians 2 Paul had *refused* to circumcise Titus.

So what in the world is he doing getting Timothy circumcised? Well, the main difference is that, unlike the Titus situation, in the Timothy situation the gospel is not at stake. In the former case, false brothers were saying, "Titus needs to be circumcised in order to be saved," whereas no one is saying that about Timothy. But there is a community of unbelieving Jews who would be easier to reach with the gospel, Paul calculates, if he accomodates culturally on this point.

Paul, sometimes in surprising ways, is willing to *adapt* and to *accommodate*. But he steadfastly refuses to *assimilate*.

In our age of identity politics, this claim—"To the Jews I became as a Jew"—is a bombshell. The world wants to shrink and reduce you to certain identity markers—your ethnicity, your class, your gender, your sexual desires, your political affiliation, and so on. But beneath all of those descriptive markers is a deeper truth: you belong to God and his people first, and this is the most important aspect about you.

What a good reminder to wear our various identity markers loosely—just as Paul wore his Jewishness loosely—as we cling to the one thing that cements our communion with other believers above all: the gospel of Jesus Christ.

Still, it is easy to go wrong here, isn't it?

## SUBVERT EXISTING CATEGORIES, CREATE NEW ONES

To be effective in our cultural moment, we must excel at asking questions.[15] We will think more about this in the next chapter. If we don't understand where a person is coming from,

> TO BE EFFECTIVE IN OUR CULTURAL MOMENT, WE MUST EXCEL AT ASKING QUESTIONS.

then we risk wasting our time (and theirs) with a message that will only be misunderstood. Raining abstract "truth bombs" on late-modern people is to risk being not just unproductive, but counterproductive: it may reinforce their misconceptions and calcify them in their resistance to gospel grace.

This is not to suggest we try to squeeze biblical truth into the mold of fallen human thought. Part of our task is to *create* categories where they don't exist. John Piper sounds an apt warning:

> As we think seriously about contextualizing the message of the Bible, let's remember that we must also labor to bring about, in the minds of our listeners, conceptual categories that may be missing from their mental framework. If we only use the thought structures they already have, some crucial biblical truths will remain unintelligible, no matter how much contextualizing we do. . . . God brings about this new seeing and understanding and believing. But he uses us to do it. So we should give as much effort in helping people have new, biblical categories of thought as we do in contextualizing the gospel to the categories they already have.[16]

Bottom line: we must *climb* into people's existing categories, excavating their cultural assumptions for points of gospel resonance; and we must also, with the Spirit's help, labor to *create* new categories that accord with supernatural truth.

In recent months, my friend Sarah and her housemate have engaged in spiritual conversations with a neighbor, Carl (not their real names). Despite growing up in church, Carl rejects the authority of the Bible, insists that Jesus is just a moral example, and dismisses the reality of hell. But his fundamental stumbling block, Sarah believes, is his view of evil and suffering. This is not surprising—his father died, then he witnessed his stepfather die, and Carl has struggled with drug addiction for years. "It is what it is," he often says about his pain. And yet, he also seems to use his story of hardship as a weapon to one-up Sarah and her housemate—or perhaps just as a way to avoid facing what they have to say about God and his Word.

So what did these women do? They remained sensitive to the particular person—a unique image-bearer of God—in front of them. They *climbed into Carl's existing category for suffering* by becoming to him, in the first place, fellow sufferers. Sarah shared about the devastating effects of an eating disorder, and her housemate was honest about her struggle to cope with her own sister's tragic death. Before, Carl had been able to dismiss these "goody-two-shoes" Christian gals; now, he ascribes to them "street cred" and seemed to respect them more. Sarah and her housemate have been gently unearthing his cultural assumption that suffering is meaningless, while seeking to *create a brand-new category of supernatural truth*. The greatest human pain, they contend, is not worth comparing to the glory that awaits Christ's people (Rom. 8:18; 2 Cor. 4:17), nor is the brokenness of this world worth comparing to the depth of our need for forgiveness of sin, which only Christ can provide (Mark 2:1–12).

The conversations continue, and Carl's story isn't over. Sarah and her housemate remain intentional, and hopeful, because they trust a big God who does miracles in human hearts.

The apostle Paul is clear:

*The natural person does not accept the things of the Spirit of God, for they are folly to him, and he is not able to understand them because they are spiritually discerned (1 Cor. 2:14).*

In other words, nonbelievers like Carl *do not* embrace supernatural truth for one simple reason: they *cannot*. The third person of the eternal Trinity must break in, granting ears to hear and eyes to see.

## HAPPINESS QUESTS

It has been wisely said that people are not so much on truth quests as they are on happiness quests. The average nonbeliever does not roll out of bed thinking, *How can I find the truth today?* But they do think, *What will make me happy today?* As Christians, of course, we have discovered that real and lasting happiness is found only in the One who said, "I am the way, and the truth, and the life" (John 14:6).

Human history, C. S. Lewis observed, is "the long, terrible story of man trying to find something other than God which will make him happy."[17] And our privilege, as gospel communicators, is showing nonbelievers how their deepest longings and hopes are resolved only in Jesus Christ.[18]

In preparing to share your faith, be prepared to "question people's answers" (which we'll explore in chapter five) by explaining how every substitute for God is a taskmaster that will enslave you. But not Jesus. Only Jesus is a master who will free you. And whereas your idols—replacements for God—will demand and disappoint and crush you into the ground, only Jesus shows up and says, "I'll be crushed for you."

> **OUR PRIVILEGE, AS GOSPEL COMMUNICATORS, IS SHOWING NONBELIEVERS HOW THEIR DEEPEST LONGINGS AND HOPES ARE RESOLVED ONLY IN JESUS CHRIST.**

As Tim Keller often says, no created thing can satisfy your heart if you get it, or forgive your sins if you fail it.[19] But Jesus can, and will. If this is true, what a story you have to tell!

Until we see Jesus as supremely beautiful—the One for whom all things were created (Col. 1:16)—we will remain a slave to something he has made. But he loves us enough to pardon, liberate, and satisfy. And where does this good news intersect with an idol-addicted heart? At the point of substitution. We have substituted so many things for Jesus. But in astonishing grace, he substituted himself for us.

> *WE HAVE SUBSTITUTED SO MANY THINGS FOR JESUS. BUT IN ASTONISHING GRACE, HE SUBSTITUTED HIMSELF FOR US.*

If your main goal in evangelism is to hear yourself talk, especially with highfalutin biblical jargon, then many late-modern skeptics will walk—or run—away confused (at best). But if your goal is to be effective, then listen in order to understand, speak in order to be understood, and respectfully engage your fellow image-bearers in their lane of life with the best news they'll ever hear.

Otherwise, you'll just be adding static to the air.

3

# LOVE THE LOST

Had I written this book several years ago, I would have swapped the order of the next two chapters, with "Face Your Fear" coming before "Love the Lost." Why? Because I was convinced that fear was the primary obstacle to evangelism. It certainly characterized my failures to speak the gospel.

Or so I told myself. Until one day it hit me: the main thing holding me back from speaking the gospel wasn't actually the presence of fear. It was the absence of love.

Perhaps this strikes you as a rather silly distinction. As I internalized it, though, I was

> ONE DAY IT HIT ME: THE MAIN THING HOLDING ME BACK FROM SPEAKING THE GOSPEL WASN'T ACTUALLY THE PRESENCE OF FEAR. IT WAS THE ABSENCE OF LOVE.

overcome with conviction. I had been using fear as an excuse when love was my problem. It wasn't even that complicated, I realized. *If I love someone enough, I will overcome my fear and share Christ with them. But if I don't, I won't.*

So welcome to chapter three, not chapter four. We must consider the role of love before the challenge of fear.

## LOVE DRIVES OUT FEAR

This realization shouldn't have surprised me, since it is an explicit biblical principle. "There is no fear in love," the apostle John observes, "but perfect love casts out fear" (1 John 4:18). In context, John's primary focus is on the fear of divine punishment, but his words constitute a powerful argument from the greater to the lesser. If a deeply felt sense of God's love has the power to banish fear of his judgment, *how much more* can it banish lesser fears, such as human rejection? One is eternal; the other is momentary. No wonder John concludes that "whoever fears has not been perfected in love" (1 John 4:18). For fear is a love problem.

And, it turns out, applying this truth horizontally—God's fear-killing love *for* us producing fear-killing love *in* us—accords with John's train of thought. He immediately writes, "We love because [God] first loved us" (1 John 4:19).

As we prepare to witness, we must prepare to love.

## BEFRIEND

Jesus was accused of many things; one was being a "friend of tax collectors and sinners" (Luke 7:34).[20] He wasn't criticized for being a passerby or an acquaintance—but a *friend*. The Son of Man came to seek and save the lost (Luke 19:10), and he did so in the context of authentic relationships. Paul, too, modeled such "relational" or "friendship" evangelism:

> *Just as a nursing mother cares for her children, so we cared for you. Because we loved you so much, we were delighted to share with you*

*not only the gospel of God but our lives as well*
*(1 Thes. 2:7–8, NIV).*

In this portion of Scripture—"more perhaps than anywhere else in his letters," John Stott notes— Paul "discloses his mind, expresses his emotions, and bares his soul."[21] The apostle was emphatic that his team's ministry in Thessalonica wasn't some hit-and-run gospel invasion. They were happy to stay, to form friendships, to invest their lives in the lives of others.

Are we?

## TWO DITCHES

This is not always easy, of course. Good intentions can get derailed, landing us in one of two ditches. (And seldom do we suddenly swerve off the road. Most of the time our wheel alignment is simply off, and so the drift is subtle—but certain.)

The first ditch is ignoring "friendship evangelism" altogether, which can lead to *treating people as projects*. We're probably most susceptible to this when initiating gospel conversations with strangers.[22] What might it look like?

- Being a poor listener.

- Rushing too quickly to the gospel.

- Not caring enough to remember their name.

I've fallen prey to this before—treating an evangelistic encounter more like a box to be checked than a person to be loved. But Jesus never did this. He never treated a person as a burden, a mere means to an end. He understood that every human life is a miracle; every human life is fascinating; every human life bears the imprint of God. C. S. Lewis's observation is striking:

> It is a serious thing to live in a society of possible gods and goddesses, to remember that the dullest and most uninteresting person you talk to may one day be a creature which, if you saw it now, you would be strongly tempted to worship, or else a horror and a corruption such as you now meet, if at all, only in a nightmare. . . . There are no ordinary people. You have never talked to a mere mortal. Nations, cultures, arts, civilizations—these are mortal, and their life is to ours as the life of a gnat. But it is immortals whom we joke with, work with,

*marry, snub, and exploit—immortal horrors or everlasting splendors.*[23]

Evangelism is not manipulation, and we don't work in sales (2 Cor. 2:17). Nor is striking up a gospel conversation a bullet point for your spiritual résumé. Faithful witnessing requires healthy doses of social awareness, common courtesy, and authentic concern. Which is just another way of saying that faithful witnessing requires love.

The second ditch is practicing "friendship evangelism" indefinitely, which can lead to *idolizing relational comfort*. As we have seen, friendship evangelism can be a beautiful thing—so long as the friendship doesn't crowd out the evangelism. It is dangerously easy to build relationships with nonbelievers in the name of gospel witness . . . without ever getting around to gospel witness.

If the danger of the first ditch is rushing the clock, the danger of the second is assuming the clock will tick forever. "You are not worth my time" is patronizing; "We have plenty of time" is presumptuous. The first ditch is immediately tactless; the second is finally spineless.

> *FRIENDSHIP EVANGELISM CAN BE BEAUTIFUL—SO LONG AS THE FRIENDSHIP DOESN'T CROWD OUT THE EVANGELISM.*

It would be a mistake to conclude that contact evangelism—sharing Christ with strangers—is inherently impersonal and unloving. As we will see in chapter five, this approach has rich biblical precedent and has led to countless conversions over the years. Extensive time in a relationship is often evidence of love, but it's not always a precondition. You can genuinely love someone in a brief interaction, just as you can fail to truly love someone in a forty-year friendship.

## LITMUS TEST

Loving the lost is not simply a spiritual virtue. It makes practical sense, too—because where love is not felt, the message is unlikely to be heard. It's that simple. Trust is essential, in other words, and this is downstream from a sense that you actually care. Though not all clichés are helpful, one is undeniably true: people rarely care what you know until they know that you care. Failing to love someone inserts a very real obstacle in the way of establishing a genuine connection. Not only does it hinder your own efforts to impart the gospel, but it may also harden their heart toward Christians in general and make the task harder for the next believer who witnesses to them.

*WHERE LOVE IS NOT FELT, THE MESSAGE IS UNLIKELY TO BE HEARD.*

But loving the lost must never be limited to the category of practical strategy—indeed, it is the healthiest litmus test of whether *you* know the God you profess. At the outset of one of Scripture's most famous chapters, 1 Corinthians 13, Paul's words could not be more bracing:

> If I speak in the tongues of men and of angels, but have not love, I am a noisy gong or a clanging cymbal. And if I have prophetic powers, and understand all mysteries and all knowledge, and if I have all faith, so as to remove mountains, but have not love, I am nothing. If I give away all I have, and if I deliver up my body to be burned, but have not love, I gain nothing (vv. 1–3).

You may be the most intentional and consistent evangelist in the world. You may even see conversions. But God is reminding us that *if we lack love*—don't miss this—we are "a noisy gong . . . nothing . . . gain[ing] nothing." Quite simply, but profoundly, love is critical to living out all our horizontal relationships—from those we live with, to those we do life with at school or work, to everyone with whom we dare to share our faith. And lest we reduce it to a warm and fuzzy feeling, Paul goes on to flesh out this love—

> LOVING THE LOST MUST NEVER BE LIMITED TO A PRACTICAL STRATEGY— INDEED, IT IS THE HEALTHIEST LITMUS TEST OF WHETHER YOU KNOW THE GOD YOU PROFESS.

it's patient, it's kind, it's humble, it's honoring, it's not irritable, it's not quick to anger, it keeps no record of wrongs, it always protects and trusts, hopes and perseveres. A tall order indeed.

## MIND YOUR MANNERS

There's more, though, to what biblical love looks like. Contrary to modern inclinations, it certainly doesn't look like affirming people in their sin.

That's a popular, and satanic, distortion. Nor does it mean compromising truth. Love without truth is a fiction—unworthy of the name *love*.

Nevertheless, there are wrong ways to be right.

We live in the age of outrage, if you haven't noticed. It can seem as if the temperature of virtually every conversation and debate, however trivial, is set to *blazing hot*. Scripture crashes into our feverish culture with both warning and command: "Do not be conformed to this world, but be transformed by the renewal of your mind" (Rom. 12:2). If you are feeding the Perpetual Outrage Machine, you are conforming to the pattern of this world, letting it "squeeze you into its own mold."[24] Jesus would say you are like salt that has lost its saltiness (Matt. 5:13)— indistinct, unnoticeable, useless. Your gospel witness, sacrificed on the altar of worldly fury, is not just ineffective; it is *counter-effective* to the cause of Jesus Christ.

Again, none of this is to say Christians must be milquetoast, mealy-mouthed individuals who shrink back while the world stands up.[25] But our manner, our posture, and our tone matter tremendously to the One who faced all manner of unfounded accusation, yet without sin. Sadly, there is a way to approach evangelism that emits an air of disdain: "I'm right, you're wrong, and I would love to tell you about it."[26] Such a spirit might make you feel noble, but it is not Christian. And it will likely obscure the gospel from being recognized as the good news it is.

"But I'm a truth-teller!" a believer might respond. "I'm authentic. I do love people—by speaking the truth." But friend, the Bible never says that speaking the truth *is* love; it says we are to speak the truth *in* love (Eph. 4:15). Ponder that distinction—it is subtle but crucial.

> THE BIBLE NEVER SAYS THAT SPEAKING THE TRUTH IS LOVE; IT SAYS WE ARE TO SPEAK THE TRUTH IN LOVE. PONDER THAT DISTINCTION—IT IS SUBTLE BUT CRUCIAL.

In short, the *way* we communicate our faith in Jesus will either adorn and beautify the gospel we profess (Titus 2:10), or undermine it. There is no third option.

One of the most concrete ways to love well is to listen well. That's not just good advice for struggling romances; it's Emotional Intelligence 101. In fact, being listened to is so close to being loved that most people cannot tell the difference.[27] No wonder Scripture exhorts us to be "quick to listen, slow to speak" (James 1:19, NIV). How often, though, do we reverse this—and risk turning people off to the voice of God because we're too in love with our own?

> HOW OFTEN DO WE RISK TURNING PEOPLE OFF TO THE VOICE OF GOD BECAUSE WE'RE TOO IN LOVE WITH OUR OWN?

Listening well entails asking thoughtful questions. Evangelism is not spiritual interrogation; no one wants to be barraged with rhetorical questions that reek of an agenda. Rather, heed the counsel of Proverbs: "The purpose in a man's heart is like deep water, but a man of understanding will draw it out" (Prov. 20:5). Engage the person with attentive questions, praying for sensitivity and wisdom, and then take the time to carefully *listen*.

We need to speak to others as if we remember what it was like to be lost, too. In this age of outrage, a countercultural message will not be compelling without a countercultural tone.

> WE NEED TO SPEAK TO OTHERS AS IF WE REMEMBER WHAT IT WAS LIKE TO BE LOST, TOO. A COUNTERCULTURAL MESSAGE WILL NOT BE COMPELLING WITHOUT A COUNTERCULTURAL TONE.

## LESSONS FROM AN ATHEIST

Penn Jillette, a well-known magician and author, doesn't believe in God. And yet listen to his perspective on evangelism:

> *I don't respect people who don't proselytize. I don't respect that at all. If you believe that there's a heaven and hell and people could be going to hell or not getting eternal life or whatever, and you think that it's not really worth telling them this because it would make it socially awkward. . . . How much do you have to hate somebody to not proselytize? How much do you have to hate somebody to believe that everlasting life is possible and not tell them that? I mean, if I believed beyond a shadow of a doubt that a truck was coming at you, and you didn't believe it—but that truck was*

*bearing down on you—there's a certain point where I tackle you. And this is more important than that.*[28]

I might phrase things a bit differently, but don't miss the significance of this atheist's words. He goes further than implying that evangelism is the most loving thing a Christian can do. He explicitly states that remaining silent is the least loving thing you can do—indeed, it's a form of hatred.

Who in your life, right now, do you love enough to share the hope of Jesus Christ?

4

# FACE YOUR FEAR

Maybe you turned to this chapter first. I hope you'll go back and read the pages leading up to it, but I certainly get the impulse. It's no secret that one of the main reasons we shrink back from sharing our faith is because we are afraid. Perhaps it's the fear of a painfully awkward interaction; or the fear of outright rejection or embarrassment; or the fear of being unequipped—lacking a ready answer for a skeptic's objection. The list goes on.

Some of our fears may feel wimpy, but they are real. Only God knows how many gospel opportunities I have squandered due to a fear that froze me in my tracks.

But evangelism is not complicated: if we wait to share our faith until our fears have completely evaporated, we will never share it.

> **IF WE WAIT TO SHARE OUR FAITH UNTIL OUR FEARS HAVE COMPLETELY EVAPORATED, WE WILL NEVER SHARE IT.**

## HELP!

This is easier said than done. Just yesterday I overheard a coffee-shop barista remark to her colleague about my T-shirt, which featured a church name. I couldn't make out everything she said, but I heard something along the lines of, "I used to go to a Baptist church." *Boom. Gospel opportunity, baby.* What did I, your trusty author, do? I slunk back to my table and continued writing a book . . . on evangelism.

I don't always fail to speak up for the same reasons. In this case, for example, I didn't fear that the barista would ridicule me, nor that she would reach behind the counter and hurl a Richard Dawkins book at me. I think I froze simply because the situation wasn't . . . perfect. She was busy making drinks, and I'd already taken a step toward my seat. (Don't give me too much credit, though: there was nobody in line. She could have chatted for at least a moment.)

I have mastered the art of passing up *good enough* opportunities in the wait for a *perfect* one. This is not just cowardly—it's foolish. The simple fact is that sharing Christ will almost always be inconvenient. There will be *something* unideal, something about the environment prompting the Devil to whisper two of his favorite words: "Not now."

This, in fact, is one of the reasons I'm writing this book. So much evangelism literature, I'm convinced, begins too far down the field. Even if you were the most knowledgeable and eloquent communicator in your whole church, it would matter little if you weren't prepared to open your mouth when the moment arrived. Rather

> DON'T WAIT FOR THE PERFECT SCENARIO; IT'LL NEVER COME. JUST RESOLVE TO SEIZE, AND STEWARD, THE ONE GOD HAS GIVEN YOU.

than being perpetually caught on our heels, I pray this book will help us more consistently live on our toes.

Don't wait for the perfect scenario; it'll never come anyway. (We'll think about this more in the next chapter.) Just resolve to seize, and steward, the one God has given you.

## WHEN THE MOMENT ARRIVES

When the moment arrives and the door cracks—suddenly, you sense, you could redirect the conversation to spiritual things—you may feel physically miserable. Seriously. Pit in your stomach? That's normal. Racing heart? Normal again. Shaky voice? Welcome to evangelism. But these unpleasant feelings are not a signal to escape, to postpone, to kick the can down the road with a resigned sigh of "next time." No, this is the moment to face the fear head on and put it in its place: "Yes, Fear, you are real and powerful—but you are not omnipotent. You are not my king. I don't answer to you; I answer to King Jesus. I'm going to lean on him and take a step of faith."[29]

Imagine—especially if you didn't grow up in a Christian home—if the person who first spoke the gospel to you had instead been frozen by fear. What if they had concluded, *No, Lord, not me! I'm still not equipped, still not ready. Plus, the environment isn't ideal.* Where might you be today?

## DON'T DO IT ALONE

Most resources on evangelism, including this one, focus on personal evangelism. We certainly need all the help we can get. Too often, though, we neglect to also consider the unique potential and power of *corporate* evangelism.

Such neglect is not intentional; it's simply natural when we have an anemic view of the local church. Weak ecclesiology does not generate strong evangelism. In Mack Stiles's book *Evangelism: How the Whole Church Speaks of Jesus*—notice the subtitle!—he lists some benefits of corporate or communal evangelism:

- We hold one another accountable.

- We strengthen our mutual resolve.

- We learn from one another.

- We rejoice together in success and cry together in disappointment.

- We bond through shared experiences in intense situations.[30]

Perhaps you can think of more. The point is that we should, whenever possible, *congregationalize* our evangelistic efforts. I don't mean you should ask your pastor to schedule another evangelistic event; I mean you should get busy yourself—and bring others along. Any church can pull off an event or launch a program. But nurturing a contagious *culture* of evangelism—a loving, magnetic, gospel-sharing community that the world can neither understand nor explain—requires dogged intentionality and the Holy Spirit's supernatural power. It happens when a church begins to see *itself* as God's most genius plan for evangelism, and when gospel conversations with the lost become a shared way of life.

> CORPORATE WITNESS IS A GAME-CHANGER IN FACING DOWN OUR FEARS. THE WORLD, THE FLESH, AND THE DEVIL CONSTANTLY OPPOSE US. BUT WHEN WE'RE WITNESSING ALONGSIDE OTHERS, THE WIND IS AT OUR BACK.

Since difficult tasks tend to become easier when we're not alone—when we can share the load with others—corporate witness is a game-changer in facing down our fears. The world, our own flesh, and the Devil constantly oppose us in evangelism. But when we're witnessing alongside others, the wind is at our back.[31]

## THE BLINDING BUSINESS

Okay, back to the personal angle. If I've learned one thing over the years as I've stumbled along in evangelism, it's this: the interaction almost always goes better than I feared.

> IF I'VE LEARNED ONE THING AS I'VE STUMBLED ALONG IN EVANGELISM, IT'S THIS: THE INTERACTION ALMOST ALWAYS GOES BETTER THAN I FEARED.

Which makes me wonder, *Might there be someone else in the equation who is scrambling, desperately, to postpone our gospel conversations until it's too late?* When it comes to evangelism, Satan is busier than we are:

> Even if our gospel is veiled, it is veiled to those who are perishing. In their case the god of this world [that is, Satan] has blinded the minds of the unbelievers, to keep them from seeing the light of the gospel of the glory of Christ, who is the image of God. For what we proclaim is not ourselves, but Jesus Christ as

*Lord, with ourselves as your servants for Jesus'*
*sake. For God, who said, "Let light shine out of*
*darkness," has shone in our hearts to give the*
*light of the knowledge of the glory of God in*
*the face of Jesus Christ (2 Cor. 4:3–6).*

The Devil is busy keeping sinners from opening
their eyes, and he does so by keeping *you* from
opening your mouth. He knows he can prevent
sight if he can simply prevent speech. And so he
is laser-focused on keeping us quiet—and thereby
shielding the lost from spiritual light, which
streams through the beautiful, hope-filled gospel
he hates.

> THE DEVIL IS BUSY KEEPING SINNERS
> FROM OPENING THEIR EYES, AND
> HE DOES SO BY KEEPING YOU FROM
> OPENING YOUR MOUTH. SATAN
> KNOWS HE CAN PREVENT SIGHT IF HE
> CAN SIMPLY PREVENT SPEECH.

## SOVEREIGN HOPE

If I did not believe God was sovereign over all
things, I would have no motivation to share my
faith. Why? Because God describes every human
heart in its spiritually fallen state as "dead in . . .

trespasses and sins" (Eph. 2:1). We dare not substitute a tamer word.

And yet Jesus summons his followers to be fishers of men (Matt. 4:19; cf. Jer. 16:14–16). How, then, can we ever hope to rescue spiritual corpses?

Because someone else gives them life. Remember Lazarus? His physical state was our spiritual state—until a voice from outside the tomb defibrillated his heart and breathed life into his lungs. Likewise, the world is a spiritual graveyard. Our job is to walk through the cemetery and speak to caskets. God's job is to crack them open.[32]

> THE WORLD IS A SPIRITUAL GRAVEYARD. OUR JOB IS TO WALK THROUGH THE CEMETERY AND SPEAK TO CASKETS. GOD'S JOB IS TO CRACK THEM OPEN.

Many misunderstand this high view of God's sovereignty in salvation—as if he drags people into the kingdom, kicking and screaming against their will. But the picture the Bible paints isn't like that at all. Imagine humanity—dead toward God but alive toward sin—sprinting toward what they're convinced is the beach. Everyone is wearing blindfolds, so they can't see what's really ahead: hell. And those who've already been rescued—believers in Jesus—are on the sidelines, shouting out in love, "Stop! Turn! You're going to perish!" Yet the blind, unbelieving rush of people only shouts back: "Oh be quiet, religious fanatics. We're not going to perish. We're going to the beach! We can feel it getting warmer now . . ."

But here's what happens. The God of mercy intervenes and begins removing blindfolds. When someone finally sees where they're actually heading, what do they do? They *freely* turn and run the other direction with joy. God doesn't make us come against our will. He makes us willing to come.

And here's the liberating lesson for us: we are not in the blindfold-lifting business! We cannot unblind a single mind or heart. Our job is to simply hold out Christ; God's job is to lift the blindfold. Who is someone in your life right now—someone with whom you will interact soon—who needs to hear the gospel? Resolve to speak to them, and ask the Spirit to send a blaze of light into their darkened heart. What if, unbeknownst to either of you, they have an appointment with him? What if, for the first time in their life, they see their need for salvation in Jesus Christ—and reverse course and run into his arms? What if the God of glory is about to remove their blinders?

> PEOPLE WHO REJECT THE GOSPEL ARE NOT FINALLY REJECTING US; THEY ARE REJECTING GOD.

*This* is the antidote to fear. For people who reject the gospel are not finally rejecting us; they are rejecting God. We are just mail carriers delivering his message.

## STAND-ALONE GOD

I'm so grateful that my college campus minister, Dan Flynn, loved to emphasize these twin truths from Scripture: "God can" and "God cares."[33] I didn't realize it at the time, but in those simple words he was distinguishing biblical Christianity from every other religion on the market. Protestant liberalism, for example, offers a God who is "good," but not great. He cares, but he can't. He's a nice buddy, an experienced life coach, even a world-class psychotherapist, but ultimately he's just "the man upstairs." Meanwhile, religions such as Islam offer the opposite: a God who is "great," but not entirely good. A God who can, but perhaps doesn't care.

When we open our Bibles, though, something unprecedented happens. It's stunning, really. We encounter a living Lord who is both great and good, sovereign and kind, who can and who cares.

If God were *only* good, I would climb into bed—and enter every evangelistic encounter—frightened. How could I trust the power of someone who, bless his heart, means well and is doing his best? But I would also be frightened if he were *only* sovereign. What assurance is there in knowing he's mighty if he's not merciful? What comfort is there in a deity who doesn't care enough to plunge into human pain, and rescue us? What hope is there in a God without scars?

## THE LAMB IS MY SHEPHERD

In Luke 12, Jesus exhorts his disciples not to be anxious, since their Father in heaven is simultaneously great and good. Then he utters one of the most beautiful statements in all the Gospels: "Fear not, little flock, for it is your Father's good pleasure to give you the kingdom" (v. 32).

Did you catch it? Shepherd. Father. King.
One tiny verse, three massive truths. The
God we meet on the pages of Scripture—and
only that God—is the Shepherd who seeks us,
the Father who adopts us, and the King who
loves us.

> YOU MAY BE AFRAID IN
> EVANGELISM, BUT YOU WILL
> NEVER BE ALONE.

And two thousand years ago, in the Lord Jesus
Christ, the shepherd King became the Lamb
slain. As comforting as it is to hear "the LORD is
my shepherd" (Ps. 23:1), there is an even better
promise: the Lamb is my shepherd (Rev. 7:17).
And just before he ascended to glory, he left
us with this indomitable assurance: "Behold,
I am with you always, to the end of the age"
(Matt. 28:20).

You may be afraid in evangelism, but you will
never be alone.

## UNBROKEN STREAK

Do you know what is the most repeated command
in the whole Bible? "Fear not." Clearly, God knew
we would need constant reminding.[34]

Human history is the long story of God's faithfulness to scaredy-cats. He has never failed one of his own—and he won't end his streak with you. Hasn't he been faithful to you over the course of ten thousand yesterdays? You can trust him to carry you in that gospel opportunity tomorrow.

5

# START TO SPEAK

"Preach the gospel at all times; if necessary, use words."

This well-known quote, misattributed to Saint Francis of Assisi, is both clever and catchy. There's only one problem: it's not biblical. While it may admirably aim to highlight that *all of life is worship*, it wrongly implies that words are secondary to works. Or optional altogether.

Evangelism—communicating the good news of Jesus Christ—always requires words. To be sure, Christians are called to *adorn* the gospel with actions (Titus 2:10), but our actions are not the gospel. No amount of righteous living can replace the necessity of verbally proclaiming what God has achieved through Christ.

This has been a book about *preparing* for evangelism more than the task itself. (There are plenty of excellent books on that; see my list of recommendations at the back.)

And yet this little book would be incomplete without this chapter. After all, someone could master everything we've discussed—grasping the gospel, checking their context, loving the lost, facing their fear—and never actually get around to *speaking*. "Pre-evangelism" is vital, but the prefix is there for a reason. It's not the real thing. Indeed, if we're not careful, we can pre-evangelize people into hell.[35]

## THE FIRST CONVERSATION

If you're afraid to share your faith, you're in good company. So were the earliest Christians. These were not comic-book heroes—men and women of superhuman valor and strength. They were ordinary folks like us.

In Acts 4, Peter and John were arrested and warned to cease and desist from speaking Christ's name, "in order that it may spread no further among the people" (v. 17). After being released and returning to their spiritual family, for what did the trembling assembly pray? "And now, Lord, look upon their threats and grant to your servants to continue to speak your word with all boldness" (v. 29).

The apostle Paul, who penned a third of the New Testament, ministered to Corinthian pagans "in weakness and in fear and much trembling" (1 Cor. 2:3). And he concluded his letter to the Ephesians requesting prayer for one specific thing:

*Pray also for me, that whenever I speak, words may be given me so that I will fearlessly make known the mystery of the gospel, for which I am an ambassador in chains. Pray that I may declare it fearlessly, as I should (Eph. 6:19–20, NIV).*

In the weighty endeavor of evangelism, prayer must never be an afterthought. It is not a nice accessory or optional add-on. It is central to the mission and critical to the task. We are in a war, after all. The enemy is real. The stakes are high. Eternal destinies hang in the balance.

It's great to know we serve the ultimate commander-in-chief, sovereign in the heavens. It's even better to know we can talk with him.

But do we?

It may be uncomfortable to admit, but our prayerlessness reveals our pride. H. B. Charles puts it simply:

> *Prayer is arguably the most objective measurement of our dependence upon God. Think of it this way. The things you pray about are the things you trust God to handle. The things you neglect to pray about are the things you trust you can handle on your own.*[36]

When we don't pray, we are not just neglecting a spiritual discipline.[37] It is far more serious than that. We are giving ourselves a promotion we don't deserve. We are daring to play God.

## PRAY TOGETHER

Private prayer is nothing short of our lifeline to our heavenly Father. Most of us know that. But just as we underestimate the value of corporate evangelism, I fear we similarly underestimate the value of corporate prayer. In a radically individualistic age, I believe it's time to *congregationalize* our prayer lives.

> **WHEN WE DON'T PRAY, WE ARE GIVING OURSELVES A PROMOTION WE DON'T DESERVE.**

Prayer is mentioned twenty-one times in the Book of Acts. Interestingly, when it shows up it is overwhelmingly public and corporate. One of my favorite things about my own church is the weekly prayer meeting, which often focuses on evangelistic requests. Yes, it can be tough to remain engaged at the end of a long day. But perhaps we shouldn't be overly surprised when we struggle to concentrate. After all, the satanic powers come to prayer meetings too, and they scramble to derail our focus by any means—even if it's just our hunger or our to-do list diverting our attention. But there's another, simpler factor: prayer is not designed to be entertaining. This doesn't jibe with a culture that has formed us to be addicted to images and screens, fascinating trivia and immediate results. No wonder prayer can feel like a slog! And so, as you approach evangelism knowing you need heaven's power, it may be time to lean into your congregation's prayer life.

Don't assume this is only for your benefit, though. To pray with your church is a profound declaration of love. How so? Megan Hill explains in her excellent book *A Place to Belong*:

> *A church prayer meeting doesn't look like much. A group of people spending an hour with their eyes closed taking turns addressing an unseen God is unlikely to draw the acclaim of the world. At best, it seems like a quaint ritual. At worst, outright foolishness. . . . The people of the world dismiss our intercessions with barely a thought. But though they don't know it, the church at prayer is their very best friend. People walking in darkness have no better ally than a group of believers on their knees, united in the work of pleading for the light of Christ to shine in their undying souls.*[38]

As God's people, we advance his kingdom on our knees. When it comes to evangelism, a faithful church is a praying church.

It has been said that life's two greatest privileges are to speak to God on behalf of others, and to speak to others on behalf of God. And that's the proper order: after we've talked to the Lord about the lost, the time has come for us to talk to the lost about the Lord.

# SPEAK TO THAT STRANGER

In chapter three, we noted some of the dangers inherent in "contact evangelism"—striking up gospel conversations with strangers. Among other things, it can tempt us to treat people as projects. Building a friendship with a nonbeliever—and taking the time to earn their trust—is almost always preferable. But life is short and we are finite. It's simply not possible to befriend the vast majority of the nonbelievers we meet. It is possible, though, to look for spiritual inroads in everyday life.

When I was in college, my campus ministry would often gear its outreaches around contact evangelism. This would sometimes elicit eye-rolls from the friendship-evangelism-only crowd, who thought our approach was cold, impersonal, even deceptive.

Any good thing can be abused, of course, and contact evangelism can certainly end up being unloving and unhelpful. But it doesn't have to be. In fact, this method is explicitly modeled in Scripture.

In John 4, for example, Jesus strikes up a conversation with a woman beside a well. Not only is she a complete stranger, she's someone he "should" avoid since she's a woman and a Samaritan (a double no-no). Nonetheless, Jesus goes out of his way to meet her, and he turns their "natural" chat about water into a "spiritual" one about himself. He doesn't waste much time, either—moving from "Will you give me a drink?" (v. 7, NIV) to "If you knew the gift of God and who it is that asks you for a drink, you would have asked him and he would have given you living water" (v. 10, NIV) in the span of just three verses.

Jesus' strategy here is not a New Testament anomaly. The early church also engaged in contact evangelism:

*Day after day, in the temple courts and from house to house, they never stopped teaching and proclaiming the good news that Jesus is the Messiah (Acts 5:42, NIV).*

*On the Sabbath we went outside the city gate to the river, where we expected to find a place of prayer. We sat down and began to speak to the women who had gathered there (Acts 16:13, NIV).*

*[Paul] reasoned in the synagogue with both Jews and God-fearing Greeks, as well as in the marketplace day by day with those who happened to be there (Acts 17:17).*

The earliest Christians were eager to initiate gospel conversations with "random" persons— with whomever their sovereign God put in their path (Prov. 16:9; 20:24).

As you go about your day, then, be on your toes. Ask the Lord to arrange "divine appointments"—unforeseen encounters that may seem coincidental to you, but were on God's schedule all along. Some of my richest gospel conversations over the years have not been planned . . . by me. But God has a calendar of his own, and he delights to arrange encounters that stretch and strengthen our muscles of faith, for the good of the lost and the glory of his name.

> SOME OF MY RICHEST GOSPEL CONVERSATIONS OVER THE YEARS HAVE NOT BEEN PLANNED . . . BY ME. BUT GOD HAS A CALENDAR OF HIS OWN.

## ANSWER THEIR QUESTIONS, QUESTION THEIR ANSWERS

Back in chapter three, we noted the importance of asking good questions—drawing people out about their life stories and beliefs, their hopes and their doubts—and then listening with deliberate care. Such conversations often evoke spiritual questions.

But at some point, we must go beyond simply answering the nonbeliever's questions—we must also question their answers.[39] For even though a modern skeptic doesn't typically enter a gospel conversation "furnished" with biblical truth,

> WE MUST GO BEYOND SIMPLY ANSWERING THE NONBELIEVER'S QUESTIONS—WE MUST ALSO QUESTION THEIR ANSWERS.

their mind is not empty. There is furniture everywhere, well-worn and comfortable and loved. It's just badly out of place.

Everyone you encounter has some vision of "the good life," and some sense of how to achieve it (or why they're failing). Whether the driving ambition is career advancement, or sexual satisfaction, or financial stability, or social capital, or the picture-perfect family, or something else entirely, the Bible is clear that we seek life in things that cannot deliver. I'm reminded of God's sweeping invitation—and searching question—in the opening verses of Isaiah 55:

> *Come, everyone who thirsts,*
>     *come to the waters;*
> *and he who has no money,*
>     *come, buy and eat!*
> *Come, buy wine and milk*
>     *without money and without price.*
> *Why do you spend your money for that which*
>     *is not bread,*
>     *and your labor for that which does not satisfy?*
> *(vv. 1–2).*

Perhaps your mind travels to other passages:

> *Be appalled, O heavens, at this;*
>     *be shocked . . . declares the* LORD,
> *for my people have committed two evils:*
> *they have forsaken me,*
>     *the fountain of living waters,*

*and hewed out cisterns for themselves,*
    *broken cisterns that can hold no water*
*(Jer. 2:12–13).*

*Those who cling to worthless idols turn*
    *away from God's love for them*
*(Jonah 2:8, NIV).*

*[A bleeding woman approached Jesus for healing,*
*as for twelve long years she] had suffered much*
*under many physicians, and had spent all that*
*she had, and was no better but rather grew worse*
*(Mark 5:26).*

Every soul in the universe is after some kind of feast, some recipe for life and joy.

In Isaiah 55, God is essentially saying, "If it's not at my banquet table—if it's not *me*—then you are impoverishing your life and starving your soul to death."

Of all the images God could have used in Isaiah 55:2, why wasting money? I suspect it is because false gods always make you pay, always exact a cost, and always finally disappoint. In explaining this to a nonbeliever, you are not standing on a balcony of superiority, speaking down to them as a hopeless idolater. Instead, you are coming alongside them, assuring them that you haven't graduated from idolatry's grip either! Even Christians convince ourselves that *this* sin, *this* time is manageable—as if we are signing up for a free trial of something. *Sure, there's some risk,* we think. *I could forget to cancel the subscription. But it's worth the risk because I probably won't forget and, in the meantime, I'll have access to all this stuff.* That's how we treat false gods and substitute saviors. We assume we can dabble a bit here and manage it there. And all the while we're plunging ever deeper into debt, with compounding interest and diminishing returns.

To see the folly of an idol, then, you must recognize its faulty price tag. You assume you're getting a deal; in truth, the idol is worth far less than you think and will cost far more than you can afford. But idols are in the false-advertising business. They are like slave-traders disguised as abolitionists.[40] They promise to free you, but if you listen carefully, you can hear the sound of shackles.

In a gospel conversation, then, don't let the nonbeliever entirely set the agenda. Answer their questions, sure, but don't stop there. Also question their answers. And don't be surprised if you find some beloved idols lurking underneath.

## SEIZE THE OPPORTUNITY

In the previous chapter, I mentioned that we shouldn't wait for *perfect* situations in order to speak of Christ. Paul didn't sit around waiting for people to come to him, to enter his world and comfort zone, before he dared open his mouth. So often we pray, and hope, and *wait* (rinse and repeat)—but never act. We rightly love 1 Peter 3:15, about living in such a way that people ask us to give a reason for our hope, but do we live as if that's the Bible's only verse on evangelism? Don't get me wrong: it is great if someone approaches you and asks to hear the truth. If you're delaying boldness until that scenario, though, you're not going to have many gospel opportunities in your life.

So, again, let's not drag our feet waiting for the "ideal" situation. For instance, if you're a parent at the park, surrounded by rambunctious kids, that's not an ideal environment. But it's where God has placed you. Why not maximize the moment? When we focus on the opportunities we *have*, not the ones we wish we did, we invite the Holy Spirit to accomplish what he's great at—doing "immeasurably more than all we ask or imagine, according to his power that is at work within us" (Eph. 3:20, NIV).

I'm reminded of a quip from Mack Stiles: "It's not that evangelism has been tried and found wanting; it's that evangelism has been found difficult and left untried."[41] He's right. There is a real sense in which the greatest obstacle to evangelism is not unbelievers, nor even Satan himself. The greatest obstacle to evangelism is Christians who don't share the gospel.

> **THE GREATEST OBSTACLE TO EVANGELISM IS CHRISTIANS WHO DON'T SHARE THE GOSPEL.**

And here's the interesting thing: most lost persons you meet—likely, most whom you know right now—have never rejected the gospel. That's because they've actually never heard it. Sure, they've rejected what they *think* is the gospel. But if you ask the average person on the street to explain it, you're not going to hear Ephesians 2:8–9 with its rich declaration of salvation by grace through faith. You're probably going to get some version of moralism, some version of "I've been a decent person."

> MOST LOST PERSONS HAVE ACTUALLY NEVER REJECTED THE GOSPEL. THAT'S BECAUSE THEY'VE NEVER HEARD IT.

And yet God has placed you in their life—at this specific place and time (Acts 17:26)—for a reason. Even if you speak the gospel and they reject it, that's a win. Progress will have been made, because at least now they will finally be rejecting the real thing and not a counterfeit. Why not speak up in order to clarify the truth and give them a chance—an actual chance—to embrace the most misunderstood message of all time?

## WATCH YOUR FOCUS

In his book *Word-Centered Church*, Jonathan Leeman recounts the following story:

> *A group of American Christians in the nineteenth century planned to visit London for a week. Their friends, excited for the opportunity, encouraged them to go hear two of London's famous preachers and bring back a report.*

*On Sunday morning after their arrival, the Americans attended Joseph Parker's church. They discovered that his reputation for eloquent oratory was well deserved. One exclaimed after the service, "I do declare, it must be said, for there is no doubt, that Joseph Parker is the greatest preacher that ever there was!"*

*The group wanted to return in the evening to hear Parker again, but they remembered that their friends would ask them about another preacher named Charles Spurgeon.*

*So on Sunday evening they attended the Metropolitan Tabernacle, where Spurgeon was preaching. The group was not prepared for what they heard, and as they departed, one of them spoke up, "I do declare, it must be said, for there is no doubt, that Jesus Christ is the greatest Savior that ever there was!"*[42]

What is true of preaching is also true of evangelism. There is an old hymn by Kate Wilkinson, the final verse of which reads:

*May his beauty rest upon me,*
*As I seek the lost to win;*
*And may they forget the channel,*
*Seeing only him.*[43]

The most important factor is not our oratory or training or smarts, but the Savior to whom we point. Let's keep the spotlight on him, and watch his grace transform hearts.

## GOD LOVES TO SAVE

Don't ever forget that God loves to save sinners. Really, he loves it! The whole thing thrills him. That's why he does it so often. In the first book of the Bible, to help Abraham visualize the scope of his spiritual offspring, God doesn't point to a cluster of trees or a pile of pebbles.

> **DON'T EVER FORGET THAT GOD LOVES TO SAVE SINNERS.**

*And he brought [Abram] outside and said, "Look toward heaven, and number the stars, if you are able to number them." Then he said to him, "So shall your offspring be" (Gen. 15:5).*

*"I will surely bless you, and I will surely multiply your offspring as the stars of heaven and as the sand that is on the seashore" (Gen. 22:17).*

Stars and sand . . . as far as human eyes can see. This is not a God who is stingy with mercy.

Sure enough, the last book of the Bible pulls back the curtain to let us glimpse this promise fulfilled. The apostle John marvels:

*After this I looked, and behold, a great multitude that no one could number, from every nation, from all tribes and peoples and languages, standing before the throne and before the Lamb (Rev. 7:9).*

We often focus on the multiethnic, multicultural diversity of this multitude, which is indeed glorious. But don't miss its *size*. There are too many persons, John says, for any mortal to count. Each has a unique story. And each is present around the throne because, once upon a time, an ordinary Christian mustered up some courage and told them about the Lamb slain.

God is far more merciful than you and I are, far more generous-hearted. And what this means, amazingly, is that he is far more willing to save sinners than sinners are to be saved (cf. Ezek. 33:11; 2 Pet. 3:9).[44]

Remember: evangelism is not converting people. Faithful evangelism is simply taking the initiative to share Christ, in the power of the Holy Spirit, and then leaving the results to God.[45]

> EVANGELISM IS NOT CONVERTING PEOPLE. IT IS SIMPLY TAKING THE INITIATIVE TO SHARE CHRIST, IN THE POWER OF THE HOLY SPIRIT, AND THEN LEAVING THE RESULTS TO GOD.

Oh, how this should steel us with confidence, with excitement, with *hope* as we go about the sacred task of sharing our faith!

# CONCLUSION:
# THE HIGHEST MOTIVATION

Several years ago, I attended a ministry conference, evangelistically earnest and theologically confident. At one point, a speaker challenged us, "I want everyone to write down the answer to this question: what is the highest motivation for witnessing to people?"

I ran through the options in my head. *Obedience to Jesus? Nah, too simple. Service to the church? Nope, too obligatory. Joy for the evangelist? Maybe too selfish. Ah, got it . . .*

I scribbled my answer—*Love for the lost*—and leaned back in my chair, waiting for others to finish. After a few moments, the speaker returned to the stage and asked what we'd written. As the answers started flying, I heard my own and smiled. I sat up. He popped it like a balloon: "Love for the lost is a very important motivation, but I don't believe it's the supreme one."

And then someone voiced it: *The glory of God.*

"Yes," the speaker replied. "Nothing in the world should motivate us more than this."

Though not a profound story, to my twenty-four-year-old self it was a bombshell. The correct answer hadn't even crossed my mind.

Let's not finish this book peering at a merely human horizon. For the most fundamental axis in evangelism is vertical. John Stott captures it well:

> *The highest [evangelistic motive] is neither obedience to the Great Commission (important as that is), nor love for sinners who are alienated and perishing (strong as that incentive is, especially when we contemplate the wrath of God), but rather zeal—burning and passionate zeal—for the glory of Jesus Christ. . . . Only one imperialism is Christian . . . and that is concern for his Imperial Majesty Jesus Christ, and for the glory of his empire.*[46]

The ultimate reason we cross cultures—and cross the street—with the gospel is not love for people, but love for *God*. Note the order, for example, in Psalm 67:

> Let the peoples praise you, O God; let all the peoples praise you! (v. 3).

> Let the nations be glad and sing for joy (v. 4).

> Let the peoples praise you, O God; let all the peoples praise you! (v. 5).

The middle verse is important, but the two surrounding it are ultimate. The joy of people is downstream from the praise of God.

God's glory as our supreme motivation carries into the New Testament as well. In the apostle Peter's words:

> But you are a chosen race, a royal priesthood, a holy nation, a people for [God's] own possession, that you may proclaim the excellencies of him who called you out of darkness into his marvelous light (1 Pet. 2:9).

Our highest objective, Peter is saying, is to magnify the worth of our God by declaring the wonder of our salvation. Likewise Paul, in the passage we considered in chapter four—about the blinding work of Satan and the illumining work of the Spirit—goes on to say, "But we have this treasure in jars of clay, to show that the surpassing power belongs to God and not to us" (2 Cor. 4:7). The treasure is the gospel; we are just the clay jars holding it. Think about it: if the treasure were housed in something beautiful (like fine china) or something strong (like iron), it would be easy for a neighbor to conclude that any apparent "surpassing power" belongs to *us*, not to God. But we're not impressive containers. We're not iron, and we're not fine china. We are pots of dirt, brittle and plain.

> OUR INADEQUACY IS NOT A LIABILITY—IT IS THE POINT. THE WEAKNESS WE FEEL IS A PLATFORM FOR CHRIST'S MIGHT TO SHINE.

Believers, there is news residing within us that's worth more than all the jewels beneath the earth. Everywhere we go, we are transporting treasure. Our inadequacy is not a liability—*it is the point*. For the weakness we feel is a platform for Christ's might to shine.

Or consider again John's vision, as recounted in the Bible's final book:

*And they sang a new song, saying,*

*"Worthy are you to take the scroll*
*and to open its seals,*
*for you were slain, and by your blood you*
*ransomed people for God*
*from every tribe and language and people*
*and nation,*
*and you have made them a kingdom and*
*priests to our God,*
*and they shall reign on the earth"*
*(Rev. 5:9–10).*

It is difficult to imagine a grander purpose for anyone than being ransomed from sin and reigning forever over a remade world. And yet, there *is* a grander purpose. Brilliant as such realities are, they are like background music to eternity's greatest hit: "Worthy are you . . . for you were slain." A believer's redemption is infinite in beauty, massive in scope, eternal in length, and yet . . . so much more. For above all else, it's meant to magnify that *one main thing*: the renown of God. No wonder, after John glimpses this diverse multitude, the spotlight dramatically shifts from us to someone greater:

> And I heard every creature in heaven and on earth and under the earth and in the sea, and all that is in them, saying,
>
> "To him who sits on the throne and to the Lamb be blessing and honor and glory and might forever and ever!" (Rev. 5:13).

In his classic book on world missions, John Piper opens with a striking observation. I have simply replaced "missions" with "evangelism." Ponder the significance of these words:

> Evangelism is not the ultimate goal of the church. Worship is. Evangelism exists because worship doesn't. Worship is ultimate, not evangelism, because God is ultimate, not man. When this age is over, and the countless millions of the redeemed fall on their faces before the throne of

*God, evangelism will be no more. It is a temporary necessity. But worship abides forever.*[47]

As we dive into the privilege of sharing our faith, let's not miss the forest for the trees. It isn't the *work of* evangelism—but rather the *worship in* evangelism—that matters most. It is dangerously easy to get so caught up in good strategies for grasping the gospel, checking our context, loving the lost, facing our fears, and starting to speak that we lose sight, somewhere along the way, of the God who is the reason for it all.

Evangelism has an expiration date. But John's vision heralds a celebration that will never end. Forgiven sinners will bask in the *evangel*—the good news of Christ—forever and ever on a new earth. As an act of worship to your King, who will you invite?

# APPENDIX:

# TWELVE VERSES FOR FIGHTING FEAR

It shouldn't surprise us that God's Word is replete with verses that speak directly to one of our besetting tendencies: fear. Here are twelve Bible passages that have proven particularly helpful to me in approaching evangelism. What if you memorized one per week for the next three months? What might that do to fortify your heart, to calm your fears, to help you speak truth in love? As Paul told Timothy, "All Scripture is breathed out by God and profitable for . . . training in righteousness, that the [servant] of God may be complete, equipped for every good work" (2 Tim. 3:16–17). *Every good work.* Sharing our faith is no exception.

---

## PSALM 56:3–4

*When I am afraid,*
    *I put my trust in you.*
*In God, whose word I praise,*
    *in God I trust; I shall not be afraid.*
    *What can flesh do to me?*

## PROVERBS 29:25

*The fear of man lays a snare,*
    *but whoever trusts in the Lord is safe.*

## ISAIAH 8:12–13

*Do not fear what they fear, nor be in dread. But the Lord of hosts, him you shall honor as holy. Let him be your fear, and let him be your dread.*

# ISAIAH 41:10

*Fear not, for I am with you;*
*be not dismayed, for I am your God;*
*I will strengthen you, I will help you,*
*I will uphold you with my righteous right hand.*

# JOHN 15:5

*I am the vine; you are the branches. Whoever abides in me and I in him, he it is that bears much fruit, for apart from me you can do nothing.*

# ACTS 18:9–10

*And the Lord said to Paul one night in a vision, "Do not be afraid, but go on speaking and do not be silent, for I am with you, and no one will attack you to harm you, for I have many in this city who are my people."*

# ROMANS 1:16

*For I am not ashamed of the gospel, for it is the power of God for salvation to everyone who believes, to the Jew first and also to the Greek.*

## 1 CORINTHIANS 2:1–5

*And I, when I came to you, brothers, did not come proclaiming to you the testimony of God with lofty speech or wisdom. For I decided to know nothing among you except Jesus Christ and him crucified. And I was with you in weakness and in fear and much trembling, and my speech and my message were not in plausible words of wisdom, but in demonstration of the Spirit and of power, so that your faith might not rest in the wisdom of men but in the power of God.*

## 2 CORINTHIANS 3:5

*Not that we are sufficient in ourselves to claim anything as coming from us, but our sufficiency is from God.*

## GALATIANS 1:10

*For am I now seeking the approval of man, or of God? Or am I trying to please man? If I were still trying to please man, I would not be a servant of Christ.*

# 1 THESSALONIANS 2:3–4

*For our appeal does not spring from error or impurity or any attempt to deceive, but just as we have been approved by God to be entrusted with the gospel, so we speak, not to please man, but to please God who tests our hearts.*

# 2 TIMOTHY 1:7

*For God gave us a spirit not of fear but of power and love and self-control.*

# RECOMMENDED RESOURCES

## SEVEN BOOKS FOR CULTURAL APOLOGETICS

- Timothy J. Keller, *How to Reach the West Again: Six Essential Elements of a Missionary Encounter* (Redeemer City to City, 2020)

- Timothy J. Keller, *Making Sense of God: An Invitation to the Skeptical* (Viking, 2016)

- Rebecca McLaughlin, *Confronting Christianity: 12 Hard Questions for the World's Largest Religion* (Crossway, 2019)

- Rebecca McLaughlin, *The Secular Creed: Engaging Five Contemporary Claims* (The Gospel Coalition, 2021)

- Joshua Chatraw, *Telling a Better Story: How to Talk about God in a Skeptical Age* (Zondervan, 2020)

- Gavin Ortlund, *Why God Makes Sense in a World That Doesn't: The Beauty of Christian Theism* (Baker Academic, 2021)

- Mark Dever and Jamie Dunlop, *The Compelling Community: Where God's Power Makes a Church Attractive* (Crossway, 2015)

## TEN BOOKS ON EVANGELISM

- Isaac Adams, *What If I'm Discouraged in My Evangelism?* (Crossway, 2020)

- J. I. Packer, *Evangelism and the Sovereignty of God* (InterVarsity, 2012)

- Mack Stiles, *Marks of the Messenger: Knowing, Living, and Speaking the Gospel* (InterVarsity, 2010)

- Mack Stiles, *Evangelism: How the Whole Church Speaks of Jesus* (Crossway, 2014)

- Mark Dever, *The Gospel and Personal Evangelism* (redesigned edition: Crossway, 2017)

- Will Metzger, *Tell the Truth: The Whole Gospel Wholly by Grace Communicated Truthfully and Lovingly* (fourth edition: InterVarsity, 2012)

- Randy Newman, *Questioning Evangelism: Engaging People's Hearts the Way Jesus Did* (second edition: Kregel, 2017)

- Rebecca Manley Pippert, *Stay Salt: The World Has Changed—Our Message Has Not* (The Good Book Company, 2020)

- Sam Chan, *Evangelism in a Skeptical World: How to Make the Unbelievable News about Jesus More Believable* (Zondervan, 2018)

- Elliot Clark, *Evangelism as Exiles: Life on Mission as Strangers in Our Own Land* (The Gospel Coalition, 2019)

# NOTES

## INTRODUCTION: NOT YOUR TYPICAL EVANGELISM BOOK

1   Matt Smethurst, *Before You Open Your Bible: Nine Heart Postures for Approaching God's Word* (10Publishing, 2019).

2   Edward T. Welch, *When People Are Big and God Is Small: Overcoming Peer Pressure, Codependency, and the Fear of Man* (P&R, 1997).

## GRASP THE GOSPEL

3   The incarnation was the fulfillment of centuries of promises—of pent-up longing and hope. Jesus is the serpent-crushing seed

of the woman (Gen. 3:15), the offspring of Abraham (Gen. 12:1–3), the son of David (2 Sam. 7:14), and Israel's long-awaited servant King (Isa. 52:13–53:12).

4   Stuart Townend, "How Deep the Father's Love for Us" (1990).

5   I am indebted to Matt Chandler for this distinction. See *The Explicit Gospel* (reprinted by Crossway, 2014).

6   For a breathtaking treatment of God's triune nature and fatherly love, see Michael Reeves, *Delighting in the Trinity: An Introduction to the Christian Faith* (IVP Academic, 2012).

7   Though difficult to determine the original source, this statement and the preceding idea of "cosmic treason" are commonly attributed to R. C. Sproul.

8   I heard this in a sermon from Tommy Nelson, longtime pastor of Denton Bible Church in Denton, Texas, though it also appears in Sinclair Ferguson, *Devoted to God: Blueprints for Sanctification* (Banner of Truth, 2016), p. 178.

9     Richard Sibbes, *The Bruised Reed* (1630; reprinted by Banner of Truth, 1998), p. 13.

10    John Stott, *The Cross of Christ* (twentieth anniversary edition: InterVarsity, 2006), p. 159.

11    Parts of this paragraph are taken from Matt Smethurst, "Is There Proof of Heaven?" (The Gospel Coalition, April 6, 2016). Available at https://www.tgc.org/article/is-there-proof-of-heaven.

12    As Sinclair Ferguson observes, "Faith will always be penitent; repentance will always be believing." See *The Whole Christ: Legalism, Antinomianism, and Gospel Assurance—Why the Marrow Controversy Still Matters* (Crossway, 2016), p. 104, note 17.

## CHECK YOUR CONTEXT

13    See Timothy J. Keller's booklet, *How to Reach the West Again: Six Essential Elements of a Missionary Encounter* (Redeemer City to City, 2020).

14    Martin Luther, *On the Freedom of a Christian* (1520).

15   Randy Newman's work is useful in this
     regard. See, for example, *Questioning
     Evangelism: Engaging People's Hearts the Way
     Jesus Did* (second edition: Kregel, 2017).

16   John Piper, "Preaching as Concept Creation,
     Not Just Contextualization" (Desiring God,
     April 10, 2008). Available at https://www.
     desiringgod.org/articles/preaching-as-
     concept-creation-not-just-contextualization.

17   C. S. Lewis, *Mere Christianity* (1952;
     reprinted by HarperCollins, 2001), p. 49.

18   Tim Keller's advice for preachers applies
     to any believer conducting an evangelistic
     Bible study: "One way to preach with a
     Christ-centered focus is to find ways to
     identify gospel 'pieces' that only Christ can
     resolve (themes), receive (law), complete
     (stories), or fulfill (symbols)." See course
     notes from Timothy J. Keller, "Preaching
     the Gospel in a Postmodern World"
     (Reformed Theological Seminary's Doctor
     of Ministry Program, January 2002), p. 35.
     Available at servantofmessiah.org/wp-
     content/uploads/2015/09/Timothy-Keller-

Preaching-the-Gospel-in-a-Post-Modern-World-Rev-2002.pdf.

19  See, for example, Timothy J. Keller, *Encounters with Jesus: Unexpected Answers to Life's Biggest Questions* (Viking, 2013), p. 38.

## LOVE THE LOST

20  This section is adapted, in part, from Matt Smethurst, "3 Ways to Share the Gospel This Week" (The Gospel Coalition, January 25, 2016). Available at https://www.tgc.org/article/3-ways-to-share-the-gospel-this-week.

21  John Stott, *The Message of 1 and 2 Thessalonians* (IVP Academic, 1994), p. 45. You can also find this quote, and further interaction with the passage, in Matt Smethurst, *1–2 Thessalonians: A 12-Week Study*, Knowing the Bible (Crossway, 2017), p. 22.

22  For a positive look at "contact" evangelism, see chapter five.

23  C. S. Lewis, *The Weight of Glory* (reprinted by HarperCollins, 2001), pp. 45–46.

24  This is how J. B. Phillips's *New Testament in Modern English* renders the verse.

25  Christian hip-hop artist Shai Linne opens his song "Taste and See" with a simple question: "The world is not subtle; why should we be subliminal?" Taken from his album *The Attributes of God* (2011).

26  I am indebted to Timothy Keller for this language: https://twitter.com/timkellernyc/status/394842579491360769.

27  David Augsburger, *Caring Enough to Hear and Be Heard* (Baker, 1982), p. 12.

28  You can watch Jillette's comments at https://www.youtube.com/watch?v=6md638smQd8.

## FACE YOUR FEAR

29  This idea of sanctified self-talk has rich biblical precedent. For example, the psalmist writes, "Why are you cast down, O my soul, and why are you in turmoil within me? Hope in God; for I shall again praise him, my salvation and my God" (Ps. 42:5–6, 11). Reflecting on this passage,

Martyn Lloyd-Jones opens his book *Spiritual Depression* with an observation: "Have you realized that most of your unhappiness in life is due to the fact that you are listening to yourself instead of talking to yourself?" See D. Martyn Lloyd-Jones, *Spiritual Depression: Its Causes and Cure* (Eerdmans, 1965), pp. 20–21.

30  Mack Stiles, *Evangelism: How the Whole Church Speaks of Jesus* (Crossway, 2014), p. 43. He also sounds this important note: "In a culture of evangelism, there is an understanding that everyone is engaged. Have you ever heard someone say, 'Evangelism is not my gift,' as if that excused him from sharing his faith? That's a kindergarten understanding of evangelism. All Christians are called to share their faith as a point of faithfulness, not gifting" (p. 54).

31  For a beautiful story of "swarm" or "mob" evangelism, see Jamie Dunlop, "The Power of Mob Evangelism" (The Gospel Coalition, October 26, 2015). Available at https://www.tgc.org/article/power-mob-evangelism. See also Mark Mittelberg, *Contagious Faith:*

*Discover Your Natural Style for Sharing Jesus with Others* (Zondervan, 2021).

32  Two verses from Jeremiah have galvanized my quaking faith over the years. The first is Jeremiah 1:12, where God says: "I am watching over my word to perform it." Communicating his truth is our job, but performing it—making it bring about something—is his. How liberating! Likewise, in Jeremiah 23:29 we read, "Is not my word like fire, declares the LORD, and like a hammer that breaks the rock in pieces?" Don't miss the point: God is guaranteeing that his Word, faithfully proclaimed, can melt and shatter the hardest heart. Dare we labor and pray for anything less? (Credit for the spiritual-graveyard image goes to Mark Dever, "How to Survive a Cultural Crisis" [The Gospel Coalition, May 27, 2013]. Available at https://www.tgc.org/article/how-to-survive-a-cultural-crisis.)

33  Portions of this chapter are adapted from Matt Smethurst, "What Are We Afraid of?" (*Tabletalk*, January 2018). Available

at https://tabletalkmagazine.com/
article/2018/01/what-are-we-afraid-of.

34  Rebecca McLaughlin, D. A. Carson, and
I discuss evangelism-related fears—and
ways to overcome them—in a brief video
conversation titled "Help! I'm Not Ready
to Share My Faith" (The Gospel Coalition,
March 5, 2019). Available at https://www.
tgc.org/podcasts/tgc-podcast/help-im-not-
ready-share-faith.

## START TO SPEAK

35  Mack Stiles, in personal conversation.

36  H. B. Charles, Jr., *It Happens After Prayer:
Biblical Motivation for Believing Prayer*
(Moody, 2013), p. 16.

37  Apathy in evangelism, John Stott warns, is
downstream from neglecting one's interior
life: "Nothing shuts the mouth, seals the
lips, and ties the tongue like the secret
poverty of our own spiritual experience. We
do not bear witness for the simple reason
that we have no witness to bear. . . . If the
Bread of life has evidently not satisfied us,

why should non-Christians suppose it will satisfy them?" See John Stott, *Evangelism: Why and How* (InterVarsity, 1962), p. 29.

38 Megan Hill, *A Place to Belong: Learning to Love the Local Church* (Crossway, 2020), p. 114.

39 I first encountered this idea in Andrew Wilson, "Tim Keller's Invitation to the Skeptical" (The Gospel Coalition, September 21, 2016). Available at https://www.tgc.org/reviews/making-sense-of-god.

40 I am indebted to John Starke for this poignant image.

41 Stiles is echoing G. K. Chesterton's famous quip. See Mack Stiles, *Evangelism: How the Whole Church Speaks of Jesus* (Crossway, 2014), p. 42.

42 This story is recounted at the outset of chapter six in Jonathan Leeman, *Word-Centered Church: How Scripture Brings Life and Growth to God's People* (Moody, 2017), p. 109.

43 Kate B. Wilkinson, "May the Mind of Christ, My Savior" (1925).

44  See J. C. Ryle's reflections on Luke 15:1–10 in *Expository Thoughts on Luke, vol. 1* (1856; reprinted by Banner of Truth, 1986).

45  I am indebted to Bill Bright, founder of Campus Crusade for Christ (now Cru), for this wording.

## CONCLUSION: THE HIGHEST MOTIVATION

46  John Stott, *The Message of Romans*, The Bible Speaks Today (IVP Academic, 1994), p. 53.

47  John Piper, *Let the Nations Be Glad!: The Supremacy of God in Missions* (third edition: Baker Academic, 2010), p. 15.

# TRUTH FOR LIFE®

THE BIBLE-TEACHING MINISTRY OF **ALISTAIR BEGG**

The mission of Truth For Life is to teach the Bible with clarity and relevance so that unbelievers will be converted, believers will be established, and local churches will be strengthened.

## Daily Program

Each day, Truth For Life distributes the Bible teaching of Alistair Begg across the U.S. and in several locations outside of the U.S. through 2,000 radio outlets. To find a radio station near you, visit **truthforlife.org/ stationfinder**.

## Free Teaching

The daily program, and Truth For Life's entire teaching library of over 3,000 Bible-teaching messages, can be accessed for free online at **truthforlife.org** and through Truth For Life's mobile app, which can be download for free from your app store.

## At-Cost Resources

Books and audio studies from Alistair Begg are available for purchase at cost, with no markup. Visit **truthforlife.org/store**.

## Contact Truth For Life

P.O. Box 398000 Cleveland, Ohio 44139
**phone** 1 (888) 588-7884   **email** letters@truthforlife.org
**truthforlife.org**